ALL AROUND THE WORLD
SWEDEN

by Jessica Dean

pogo

Ideas for Parents and Teachers

Pogo Books let children practice reading informational text while introducing them to nonfiction features such as headings, labels, sidebars, maps, and diagrams, as well as a table of contents, glossary, and index.

Carefully leveled text with a strong photo match offers early fluent readers the support they need to succeed.

Before Reading

- "Walk" through the book and point out the various nonfiction features. Ask the student what purpose each feature serves.
- Look at the glossary together. Read and discuss the words.

Read the Book

- Have the child read the book independently.
- Invite him or her to list questions that arise from reading.

After Reading

- Discuss the child's questions. Talk about how he or she might find answers to those questions.
- Prompt the child to think more. Ask: Herds of reindeer live in Sweden. Do reindeer live near you? Have you ever seen them?

Pogo Books are published by Jump!
5357 Penn Avenue South
Minneapolis, MN 55419
www.jumplibrary.com

Library of Congress Cataloging-in-Publication Data

Names: Dean, Jessica, 1963- author.
Title: Sweden / by Jessica Dean.
Description: Pogo books. | Minneapolis : Jump!, Inc., [2019]
Series: All around the world | Includes index.
Audience: Ages 7-10.
Identifiers: LCCN 2018022796 (print)
LCCN 2018023051 (ebook)
ISBN 9781641281751 (ebook)
ISBN 9781641281737 (hardcover : alk. paper)
ISBN 9781641281744 (pbk.)
Subjects: LCSH: Sweden–Juvenile literature.
Classification: LCC DL609 (ebook)
LCC DL609 .D43 2019 (print) | DDC 948.5–dc23
LC record available at https://lccn.loc.gov/2018022796

Editor: Kristine Spanier
Designer: Molly Ballanger

With acknowledgment to Dr. Tim Frandy of Western Kentucky University for his expertise in the Sámi language.

Photo Credits: Adisa/Shutterstock, cover; stocksnapper/iStock, 1; Pixfiction/Shutterstock, 3; bbsferrari/iStock, 4; Massimo Pizzotti/age fotostock/SuperStock, 5; Stock Connection/SuperStock, 6-7, 20-21; Richard Cavalleri/Shutterstock, 8-9; JohanSjolander/iStock, 10; Tsuguliev/Shutterstock, 11; Maskot/Getty, 12-13; Anders Blomquist/Getty, 14-15; Hemis/Alamy, 16-17; Lesya Dolyuk/Shutterstock, 18; Frank Chmura/Alamy, 19; bildfokus.se/Shutterstock, 23.

Printed in the United States of America at Corporate Graphics in North Mankato, Minnesota.

TABLE OF CONTENTS

CHAPTER 1
WELCOME TO SWEDEN!

Dance around a **maypole**. Pick fresh berries in the country. Walk the cobblestone streets of Gamla Stan. This town is more than 760 years old!

cobblestone

Marvel at the Vasa. This ship sank more than 350 years ago. Welcome to Sweden!

Vasa · · · · ▶

An ice hotel is in Jukkasjärvi. Artists from around the world create each room. Sun melts the hotel in April. Ice from the Torne River is used to rebuild it every year.

Drottningholm Palace

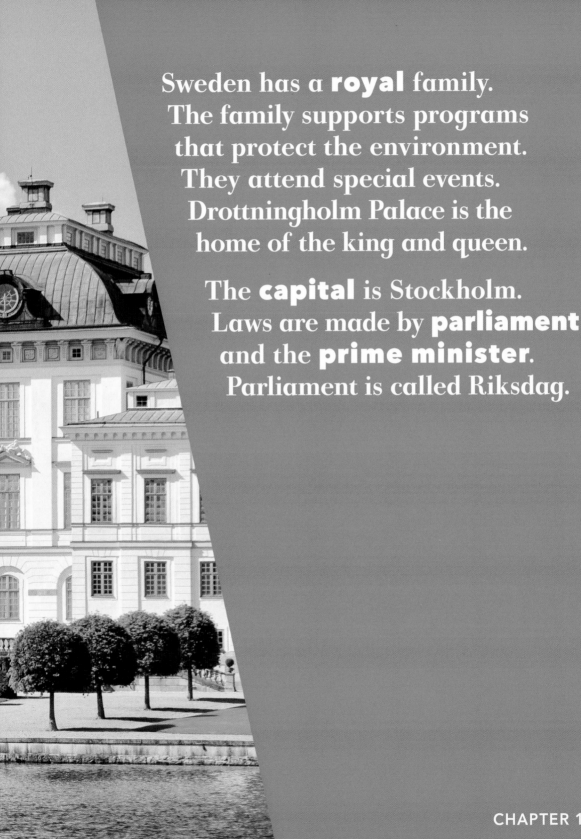

Sweden has a **royal** family. The family supports programs that protect the environment. They attend special events. Drottningholm Palace is the home of the king and queen.

The **capital** is Stockholm. Laws are made by **parliament** and the **prime minister**. Parliament is called Riksdag.

CHAPTER 2

SWEDEN'S PEOPLE

The Lapland area is inside the **Arctic Circle**. Some days in summer see 24 hours of daylight. Long summer days draw hikers. They climb the green mountains.

December brings much less sunlight. How much? Only three hours each day! Sometimes northern lights appear.

northern lights ·····▶

Swedes start school when they are seven years old. Most attend preschool for one year first. In high school, students learn a **trade**. Or they prepare for college.

Many students are in sports. They may ski, skate, or play hockey. Brännboll is like softball. Schools are closed for a week in February. Why? So families can take sports vacations!

WHAT DO YOU THINK?

Knowing more than one language is important here. Children learn Swedish at home. They learn English at school. Then they usually learn two more languages. How many languages would you like to learn?

Hallå!

Hello!

The Dala horse was once a simple toy for children. Now it is a **symbol** of Sweden. Why? People living in Dalarna have been carving these wooden horses for more than 300 years. Artists paint them with bright colors and flower patterns. They are sold all around the world.

Dala horse

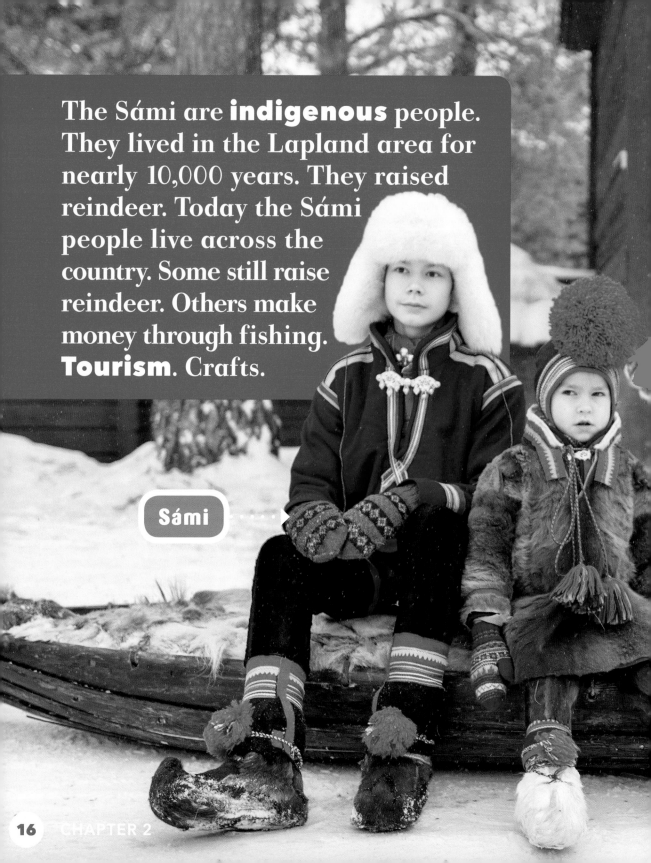

The Sámi are **indigenous** people. They lived in the Lapland area for nearly 10,000 years. They raised reindeer. Today the Sámi people live across the country. Some still raise reindeer. Others make money through fishing. **Tourism**. Crafts.

Sámi

TAKE A LOOK!

Sámi people still wear their traditional clothing. The outfits have many pieces to them.

GAHPIR
(hat)

LIIDNI
(shawl)

RISKU
(brooch)

BOAGÁN
(belt)

FÁHCAT
(mittens)

GÁKTI
(outfit)

VUODDAGAT
(shoe wrapping)

GÁPMAGAT
(shoes)

CHAPTER 3

FOOD AND CELEBRATIONS

Swedes often start the day with yogurt and toast. Lunch is served at school. Meatballs, potatoes, and jam are common for dinner. So are lighter meals such as fish with vegetables.

meatball ···▶

A Swedish feast is called a **smörgåsbord**. It is a special event for holidays. Guests choose food from a spread of dishes.

smörgåsbord

St. Lucia's Day is December 13. This marks the beginning of the Christmas season. A girl wears a wreath with candles. She leads children dressed in white robes through the streets. They carry candles and sing special songs.

Sweden is a charming country. Would you like to visit?

WHAT DO YOU THINK?

Midsummer is a summer holiday here. People have picnics. They dance around a maypole in the long hours of the sunlight. Do you celebrate a holiday in the middle of the summer? Is it similar to or different from the summer holiday in Sweden?

QUICK FACTS & TOOLS

SWEDEN

Location: Northern Europe

Size: 173,860 square miles (450,295 square kilometers)

Population: 9,960,487 (July 2017 estimate)

Capital: Stockholm

Type of Government: parliamentary constitutional monarchy

Language: Swedish

Exports: machinery, petroleum, motor vehicles, paper, clothing

Currency: Swedish krona

GLOSSARY

Arctic Circle: The area surrounding the northern part of Earth.

capital: A city where government leaders meet.

indigenous: Living or existing naturally in a particular region or environment.

maypole: A tall flower-wreathed pole that forms a center for dances.

parliament: A group of people elected to make laws.

prime minister: The leader of a country.

royal: Relating to or belonging to a king or queen or a member of his or her family.

smörgåsbord: A buffet offering a variety of foods and dishes.

symbol: An object or design that stands for, suggests, or represents something else.

tourism: The business of serving people who are traveling for pleasure.

trade: A particular job, especially one that requires working with one's hands or machines.

Sweden's currency

INDEX

TO LEARN MORE

Learning more is as easy as 1, 2, 3.

1) Go to www.factsurfer.com

2) Enter "Sweden" into the search box.

3) Click the "Surf" button to see a list of websites.

With factsurfer, finding more information is just a click away.